A Good Neighbor

Also By Robert Benson

Between the Dreaming and the Coming True
Living Prayer
Venite: A Book of Daily Prayer
The Night of the Child
The Game: One Man, Nine Innings, a Love Affair with Baseball
That We May Perfectly Love Thee
The Body Broken
A Good Life
Home by Another Way
Daily Prayer
Digging In: Tending to Life in Your Own Backyard
In Constant Prayer
The Echo Within

A Good Neighbor

Benedict's Guide to Community

Robert Benson

PARACLETE PRESS
BREWSTER, MASSACHUSETTS

A Good Neighbor: Benedict's Guide to Community

2015 Second Printing (POD)
2009 First Printing

ISBN: 978-1-55725-582-2

The Paraclete Press name and logo (dove on cross) are trademarks of Paraclete Press, Inc.

Library of Congress Cataloging-in-Publication Data

    Benson, R. (Robert), 1952-
      A good neighbor : Benedict's guide to community / by Robert Benson.
        p. cm.
      Includes bibliographical references.
      ISBN 978-1-55725-582-2
      1. Benedict, Saint, Abbot of Monte Cassino. Regula. 2. Neighborliness—Religious aspects—Christianity. 3. Christian life. I. Title.
      BX3004.Z5B46 2009
      248.4—dc22   2009006794

10 9 8 7 6 5 4 3 2

Published by Paraclete Press
Brewster, Massachusetts
www.paracletepress.com

Printed in the United States of America

This book is for
Kendra & John and Emily & Jason.

And it is for The Friends of Silence & of the Poor,
whoever and wherever you may be.

Contents

A Beginning

Love one another as I have loved you.
—The Gospel of Our Lord

*Seeking his workers in a multitude of people,
the Lord calls out and lifts his voice again:
Is there anyone here who yearns for life and
desires to see good days?*
—From the Rule of Saint Benedict

*Benedict's Rule is simply a practical manual
to give guidance to a family of brothers, an
extended household, who had to earn their
living, who were concerned with food, with
the care of visitors or the sick, with the upkeep
of buildings and land, while recognizing the
need for time to read and study—and yet
determined to make prayer the central focus,
the one priority of their lives.*
—Esther de Waal (adapted)

All of the Law and all of the Prophets can be fulfilled in two commandments," said the One Who came among us to those He walked among.

"Love God," He said. "And love your neighbor."

This book is about the second of those commandments. Any conversation about community—discovering community, living in community, nurturing community, restoring community—is, at the very core, a conversation about loving one's neighbor and being loved in return. Being loved enough in return that something like community or fellowship or common purpose takes place between us. Whether the *neighbor* in question lives across town or across the globe, down the block or down the hall, in the same town or in the same house.

———

I have never lived, and likely never will, in a community that is under the Rule of Saint Benedict, a guide for monastic communities. That is not the life to which I am called. I am called to live a life of work and family, art and prayer, in the world outside the walls of a monastery. But in the same way that I believe that those who live a life of prayer in communities intentionally made for prayer have much to teach us about prayer, I believe that the monks and nuns who live in Benedictine settings have much to teach us about community.

There is wisdom about prayer in such places that can be transposed into my life if I will take the time to read and listen and observe and wait. There is wisdom about life lived together that can also be transposed into my life, when I listen and observe and wait.

While reading and studying Benedict's Rule some time ago now, I discovered a pattern prescribed by Benedict that helped me begin to balance prayer and work and community and rest. This pattern I came to see in the life of the One Who came among us, too. Because the Rule is based on Scripture, discovering the connection of one pattern to the next did not surprise me.

These days I am seeing another pattern, one that is four-fold.

- In the beginning was the Word
  and the Word humbled Himself
  and came among us.
- Jesus showed mercy to those who
  came to Him.

- Jesus welcomed everyone,
  regardless of social standing.
- Jesus cared for those who were
  given to Him and to whom
  He was given.

This pattern is echoed in the Rule of Saint Benedict. It is a pattern that helps us discover and build and nurture and restore community in our lives. It is a pattern that helps us follow the second of the great commandments.

A Longing for Community

Keep seeking until you find.
—The Gospel of Our Lord

Open your eyes to the light that comes from God, and your ears to the voice from heaven that every day calls out this charge: If you hear his voice today, do not harden your hearts.

What is not possible to us by nature, let us ask the Lord to supply by the help of his grace.
—From the Rule of Saint Benedict

Unless we learn to live with ourselves we cannot live with others. But equally, unless and until we have learnt to live full and creatively with others we cannot hope to live with our own selves.
—Esther de Waal

I am among the shyest people you might ever meet.

One of my friends once wrote that he was so shy that if you sat next to him on a bus ride to California, he would probably not say two words to you unless you were sitting on his hat.

He could have written that sentence about me.

I have heard folks say this about their friends: "We are so close that we can go for years without seeing each other and then when we do, the conversation picks up right where it left off."

I can go for years without seeing some of my closest friends and when we finally meet again, the silence picks up right where it left off. That is how you know you are one of my best friends: we enjoy sharing silence as much as we enjoy sharing conversation.

So for me to be writing a paragraph about community much less a book about community makes me laugh at myself more than a little. Though, I have learned more about community by keeping my mouth shut than I have by talking. This is a lesson I learned from the great spiritual thinker Yogi Berra, who said, "You can observe a lot just by watching."

When I have been still and silent long enough to really see and hear, I have noticed that a deep sense of community is not easy to come by. As shy as I am I know, too, that I long for it in my own life.

In silence and observance I have also learned that most of us have this longing no matter how we live out our lives.

"We live our lives in search," writes Frederick Buechner. "We search for a self to be, we search for work to do, and we search for other selves to love."

Community is another way to say *other selves to love*, of course, and even we shy folks live our lives in search of folks to love and to be loved by in return, people who will share in the ups and downs of our journey, people who will walk beside us in the light and dark of our days. We too are hoping to find and to be found by folks with whom we have common cause and work, shared dreams and hopes, collective wisdom and experience. We too want to belong to something larger than ourselves. We too hope to be included and to be held dear and to be thought of often. The same is true of us all, the shy ones and the not-so-shy ones.

Our longing for community seems to be a part of the image of the One Who made us, a part of the divine image whispered into us when we were whispered into being in the first place. The hard part is to learn how to see and build and nurture community, and live in and out of and around and through it. A deep sense of community may not ever have been easy to achieve, but it seems especially difficult in the midst of the modern world in which we live.

In some ways, we have never been so able to be connected to each other as we are in our modern world. Technology has made it possible for us to be in touch instantly with people around the world; to hear news as it happens from one side of the globe to the other; to make a few clicks with a mouse or a couple of strokes on a keyboard and be looking at the pictures from a dinner party we attended last evening, at the terror of a wildfire in California, at the joy of a cousin's wedding in Duluth, or at a Washington parade in which a group from our neighborhood marched.

Some of us can talk to our dashboards while we are driving along the highway and tell some device inside the dashboard to call home for us, and the hidden wonder will do just that. We can invite dozens of folks to our house for a party and never have to write out an invitation or lick a stamp or answer the telephone to see if anyone is coming. We can go online and order groceries, connect to a website to buy books, and send flowers to folks we love without ever visiting a florist. The president-elect of the United States once sent me a personal note on my telephone before he gave a speech in a park in Chicago. It is an astonishing world.

We live in a world where we can live in neighborhoods for years and never know our neighbors, take our children to school for years and never meet the parents of the children they go to school with, sit in a pew next to a couple for years and never know what they do for a living, and live in a city surrounded by tens of thousands of people and never feel as though we belong.

We live in a world where information and ideas come at us at great speed, where conversations have a tendency to move quickly, where messages are instant and meanings often missed. Such a world is not exactly an easy environment in which to build community. It is not even easy to say what we mean by the word when we use it.

The word *community* comes from a Latin word and according to the fine folks who publish *The Oxford English Dictionary* (OED)—bless them, all of them—it takes a good three columns, a shade under thirty inches of very small type, to explain its meaning. When so many words are required to unpack what a word means, that word is richer than most. The word is likely to be full of subtlety and texture and depth and wonder. The word is likely to be hard to pin down and, at least in the case of *community*, hard to find in the world.

Through all of the definitions and examples and references the OED provides, there seem to be two woven threads.

The first thread comes from the original roots of the word. The earliest definitions yield up words like *fellowship* and *social intercourse*. There are phrases like *community of relations or feelings* and *life in association with others. Common character* and *identity* are mentioned.

These are the kinds of words and phrases we call to mind, I suppose, whenever we talk about our desire to live with some greater sense of community in our lives. We have a common longing for deeper fellowship with those with whom we live and work and worship. We have a longing for being known more intimately by those with whom we identify, with whom we are connected—our families, our neighbors, our friends, our coworkers, our fellow parishioners.

The second thread comes to us from medieval times. During those days the word *community* came to be used for a body of people organized into a political or geographical or social unity.

The word began to be used to describe a body of men or women living together and practicing, more or less, a community of shared goods and possessions—villages, towns, neighborhoods, trade, and church communities.

Some of those communities were the monasteries founded by Saint Benedict and those who lived under what is called the Rule of Saint Benedict.

7

Benedict was living as a solitary in a cave some thirty miles from Rome when a group of monks asked him to be their abbot. His first attempt to live in community with other monks did not work out so well, and Benedict returned to his cave. A few years later he was asked by another group, and as a result, he set up twelve monasteries of twelve monks each.

Having learned a thing or two from his first attempt to be abbot for a crowd of monks—failure is one of the ways we get wiser, even if we are on the road to becoming a saint—Benedict wrote a Rule to guide the individual and collective lives of these other monks. The Rule not only guided their prayer, the Rule regulated every part of their life together—prayer and work and community and rest. It shaped the way they ate, the way they took in new monks, the way they assigned roles based on positions of authority, the way monks were disciplined, and so on.

Some fourteen hundred years later, the Rule of Saint Benedict is the foundational Rule for Christian monastic communities around the world. The Rule gives the longing for community an opportunity to be fulfilled in monastic settings.

The people who live in the community hold property and goods in common, they are obedient to the authority of the abbess or abbot, and they do their assigned chores as part of a common effort to contribute to the overall purposes and well-being of the community.

They become a community in both senses of the word—a group sharing fellowship and common character as well as a group belonging to a particular place.

They live together, work together, and pray together every day. Every day of the year. In fact, every day of their lives.

Perhaps if I could define my community as if I were living in a Benedictine monastery and my world was populated mostly by those who lived within its walls and who were as committed and bound to me as I was to them, the longing for community, for deep fellowship, for knowing and being known might become easier to satisfy. Though, I do not mean to suggest living with other folks would necessarily be easier if I lived in a monastic setting; the witness of the saints is enough to dispel any such notion. Saint Benedict himself left his first monastery because the monks were plotting to kill him. And he was the abbot.

I heard spiritual director Elizabeth Canham tell stories about the monastic community for whom she directed a retreat center for many years. She mentioned in passing that the member of the community you are going to have the hardest time getting along with is always in residence in the community before you even get there. The One Who made you and Who has brought you there will see to it.

I am happy to know that some of the people of prayer known as monks and nuns can be challenging to get along with. This is not to say, of course, that they are not people of prayer or even that I myself might not yet become a person of prayer. I am especially happy to know this to be true on the days I am particularly challenging to get along with. Or on days when I am having trouble with someone who can likewise be a challenge. For the One Who made us has seen to it that I have one or two of those folks in the communities in which I live.

I never have lived in a monastic setting of any sort, though I do know enough to understand that the challenges and obstacles and struggles to fulfill our longing for deep communion with others may be different ones. And I know that such communities are no better or worse than the ones the rest of us live in; they are simply made up of people who are called to that way of life. And I am not called to live the life monastics live.

What I *am* called to do is be as deeply engaged in and present to and in communion with those to whom I have been given and who have been given to me. Which is what it will mean for me to fulfill my longing for community.

I also have learned from Elizabeth Canham that whatever are the challenges that come with our communities, we are to meet those challenges with as much joy and determination as possible.

One of the challenges to fulfilling the longing I have for community does not come from having no community at all. In fact, in some ways, the opposite is true.

The challenge comes from living, as most all of us do, in several communities at the same time. Communities that do not happen to be in the same place. The resulting challenge is not insignificant but neither is it insurmountable.

First, I live in the community that is my family. My children are grown now and live only a few minutes away, and a fair number of the folks who make up our extended family live in and around the city, too. I am a poet, not a math whiz, but by my rough calculation, we reside in eight houses stretched out over 720 square miles, an area not exactly conducive to giving each other a pat on the back or saying hello while passing each other on the way to prayers or to a meal. We have times for and ways of keeping in touch, but we do not see each other often.

One of those houses is where I live with the woman to whom I am married. We do have the chores we perform together around the house and we have the kind of long conversations about making books one would expect to take place where a writer and a literary agent live, but I do not actually do my work with the community I live with.

The second community in which I live out the majority of the days of my life is a small community called Sunnyside. Sunnyside is the name for the three hundred or so houses which occupy the eighteen square blocks we call home. Sunnyside is the old name for the neighborhood. The new name is not as cool sounding to me. And according to the neighborhood association, when you use the new name, you take in another twenty square blocks and another few hundred houses. Being as shy as I am, after ten years or so, I still have not met everyone who lives in Sunnyside.

But we do know a lot of folks, and we are invited to sit on a lot of porches and share a lot of meals in a lot of backyards. We try to always go to the summer concerts in the park a few blocks away so we can see everyone and catch up on the news. There are two coffee shops and four restaurants in Sunnyside, and when we walk we meet people we know every five minutes. Sometimes I wish there were bells to call us to stop and pray together in Sunnyside. And as much, like the monastics, as I have in common with these folks, we do not work together or hold our property in common. Yet we are a community.

I am also a member of the cathedral parish in our town, and have been for ten years or so—proudly so, I might add. The cathedral is a fine place to worship, and after some conversational challenges largely connected to my shyness—I attended every Sunday for a year, for example, before I finally went out the back door and shook hands with one of the half dozen or so priests who were waiting after the service— I have now met enough of my fellow parishioners to bear witness that the parish is made up of generally fine folks.

And the two thousand or so of us who make up this community also live all over the six counties that make up our metro area, and we all drive downtown to share our worship and then drive back to our neighborhoods to live our lives. We work in other communities and we hang on to our own goods. Except for those few moments each week when we drive downtown for the Sunday service, our prayer is said in private. We say it alone together, one might say, which is no small thing but it affects our sense of community.

But according to the catechism, we are a community of faith. And I believe we are.

And if you could see and hear us gathering up together for the Holy Eucharist on a Sunday morning or gathering up at an Evensong on an evening in Lent or pounding nails into a house for Habitat for Humanity or collecting things on behalf of a thrift shop for the poor at St. Luke's, you would think so too.

For the record, I am also a member of the local literary community, a part of the national publishing community as a whole, and an alumnus of a spiritual formation community that has now grown to more than a thousand members (I have even met a third of them). And, as has become increasingly obvious in our global age, obvious even to a shy Luddite, I happen to be a citizen of the world.

For a shy person, one who shares a house with only one other person, works alone in a little building in the back garden, and has to make up reasons to leave the house, I certainly seem to live a life full of folks. There is a sense in which I have so many communities of which I am a part that living in community should be as easy a thing to do as there possibly could be. But if, in fact, someone offers me a chance to be in community, I am going to think long and hard. I have so many associations now I can hardly stand it.

What I long for now, rather than additional communities, is an abiding sense of deep fellowship and communion with the people with whom I am currently sharing my life, no matter where they live or how often I see them.

I am coming to believe that for many of us, some of the difficulty in living our lives with any deep sense of fellowship and communion begins not with the fact that we are a part of no community at all, but rather that we are a part of so many of them.

I have read enough about and talked to enough people in monastic communities to know there are unique challenges to living in them. There are also some challenges to living *in* community for those of us who do not live in a *single* community. The first is to remember that we are called to these communities and if we answer the call to help shape community, these are the places where we are to be doing so.

In the prayer book I use most of the time, these words are said toward the end of morning prayer, before intercessions or petitions or thanksgivings are to be offered up: "We offer our prayer for those with whom we share the Journey, those who have been given to us and to whom we have been given." I have come to love those words.

Those words help me see more clearly how true it is that I have found other selves to love. The truth is I now have so many other selves to love—family and friends, fellow parishioners and poets, business associates and neighbors—I can hardly stay in touch with them all. And there is no common rule for being in touch with them or praying with them or working with them. My being in community with them is made more difficult, almost daily, by the simple fact that we all live in such different ways and in such different places and under such different circumstances.

How then to be in community with these communities to whom I have been given? How then to be present to and pray with those who have been given to me? How then to love them and be loved by them in return?

This is the place where the good Saint Benedict himself begins to speak to me, and perhaps to us all.

Some of what Benedict has written in his Rule is clearly for people who are responding to a different calling. There are regulations for how many letters a monk may receive in a year, what time breakfast should be served during the harvest season, what to do with the summer robes when the time comes for the winter ones, what time to stop reading in the mornings during Lent. These bits of the Rule are for times and places and communities of which I am not a part.

Yet, some of the lessons Benedict learned and taught within a small group of monks all those years are lessons we moderns who long for community would do well to listen to. Lessons about mercy and humility, about suffering and confession, about hospitality and caring and welcome, about a kind of spiritual posture that may create the room for a deeper sense of community to grow in the communities into which we have been called—all of the communities of our calling.

What I am seeking now, in the following pages, is the guidance that might be there in the Rule for someone like me and someone like you, people who do not live with the people we work with, do not pray with the people who live in the house next door or in the next block, and do not see the people we work with outside of the place where we work.

I am in search of what the Rule can teach us about nurturing fellowship with people with whom we often share only a part of our lives rather than most of our lives. I am hoping to discover some of what the Rule has to say about building a sense of community with people with whom we share only a small portion of our lives in common.

Is there a way for us to read the lines of a Rule written for a certain kind of community and discover what is to be found in the lines and between those lines that can help us learn how to more fully live in community with the myriad of communities to whom we moderns have been given?

I believe there is.

In the end, our longings are less about how we find community and more about how we live in relationship to those to whom we have been given.

We know to whom we have been given, even if some of the names and faces change as we go in and out of the different seasons of our lives.

Some of the people who lived down the block, ones we loved the most, have now moved away. Or our children—the ones that writer Khalil Gibran once called "the sons and daughters of life's longing for itself"—do what we had thought they might do all along, grow up and then move away to live their own lives.

Sometimes the *where* of our life changes. We change jobs, we change towns, we change parishes. We begin to work with other people who come to take the place of the people we had worked with for so long. We move into a new house and realize we know no one on the block and have to start over with a portion of our life in community. A priest leaves and a new one comes, and the crowd of people with whom we pray and worship begins to shift and change.

The longing that never changes is the one for deep engagement with and presence to those to whom we have been given. Our longing to live in communion with them, to share deeply in the part of our life we hold in common with them, to be in community with them no matter the distances that separate us or the circumstances that have brought us to each other—these longings have been with us for all time past. And will be with us for all time to come.

From out of the all time past speaks the wisdom of Benedict, wisdom that can teach us much about community in the time to come.

Heroic Humility

Whoever exalts himself shall be humbled, and whoever humbles himself shall be exalted.
—The Gospel of Our Lord

The first step of humility is unhesitating obedience, which comes naturally to those who cherish Christ above all.

Only in this are we distinguished in the sight of God: if we are found better than others in good works and humility.
—From the Rule of Saint Benedict

We are being asked to walk free of the structures and aspirations of contemporary society while still living in the midst of it.
—Esther de Waal

If one is going to wander into a discussion about community that includes some of Saint Benedict's ideas about the subject—which is obviously what you have wandered into here—then he or she is not going to get very far without running into Benedict's strong feelings about humility. The good saint seems to believe humility is the proper posture for those who would live with others. In fact, the more I read the Rule, the more I get the impression he believes community may not even be possible without humility.

And on a regular basis, the liturgy at the cathedral community to which I have been given reinforces what the saint has to say.

———

At our house we like a ceremony.

We like tea in the afternoon with all of the silver and the attendant rigmarole. We like to have our children with us at the house for the Christmas feast—everyone dressed up for dinner, roast beef and old china and toasts all around, and little prizes for everyone after the dessert.

When we go to baseball games, we go early in order to be on time for the ceremony known as batting practice. We like to watch the grounds crew prepare the field before the game and we always stand to sing during the seventh-inning stretch. When the summer comes to a close, we call our friends and have one last garden party before the weather turns cool. The late September party is a mirror of the garden party we threw a few months before to celebrate the spring's arrival.

Most of all we like liturgical ceremony.

We like the processional that opens almost every service at the cathedral. We like to watch the chancel participants pause and bow before they climb up the steps to the chancel. We especially enjoy what a choir member once told me is referred to as the holy figure eight, the great parade on high holy days in which the priests and the choir keep going around the room, up one aisle and down another, around and around, while chanting and singing and ringing bells and all the rest.

We love to watch babies being hauled to the baptismal font to be sprinkled with water and welcomed into the household of faith. We have even been known to go over and stand in the aisle near the baptismal font so we can see the proceedings better, even if we do not know the baby or the parents. We like to be in church on Good Friday when the altar is stripped in silence, and we like to be there on Easter morning when the astonishment of the resurrection story fills the room to near bursting with joy. We like to be there for the simple and quiet Christmas morning liturgy when almost no one attends and every sound echoes off those great hallowed walls and columns and windows, and the wonder of the Light of the world among us seems real and true.

The Nazarenes, among whom my wife and I were raised, are not very big on liturgical ceremony in their church services. These ancient rites are simply not a part of their practice or tradition. My own spiritual journey took me off wandering around in the woods for a bit, and when I came out into the light again, I found my place among a crowd of people who like their ceremony.

The crowd includes the woman to whom I am married. Her favorite service at the cathedral each year is on Maundy Thursday during Holy Week. This is the service at which we remember the gathering up of Jesus and his disciples on the night, as the liturgy goes, "he was handed over to suffering and death." Maundy Thursday is the service during which people wash each other's feet, in remembrance of the most humble of acts that Jesus performed for his friends.

My wife's next favorite time to gather with the cathedral community is Ash Wednesday.

I myself would choose Christmas—the celebration of the coming of the Light of the world. I choose a liturgy full of joy and wonder, and she chooses a liturgy of humility and repentance.

Based on her humility alone, not to mention her good works as opposed to mine, I am reasonably certain she would be preferred by Saint Benedict to me, even though I am the one who has been studying him for years.

One day I said to myself, "I have some good news for you, Robert. I have figured out one of the key ingredients for living in community, according to Saint Benedict.

"The bad news, Robert, is that the key ingredient is humility."

I am not sure I am happy about the news, but I am pretty sure I am reading the news correctly. *Humility* is not a particularly popular word for us twenty-first-century Americans. We are daughters and sons of the famously and furiously independent souls who built this country, and we have been taught over and over that we are destined to be masters and mistresses of our own fates.

A writer I know used to say he was trying to be more humble. "If I had humility, I would be perfect," he would say. He also used to say it was hard to be humble when you were as talented as he was. He made both of these statements with his tongue planted firmly in his cheek.

Now I expect someone living inside a monastic community might argue that the key word for living in community in such a context would be *obedience*. This may be right, I do not know. Not having an abbot or an abbess on the premises of the communities of which I am a part, or even a written rule signed on to by all of the people in all of those communities in which I operate, *obedience* seems an elusive term. But I venture to say one cannot get to obedience without going through humility.

The context and shape and form of community life is different for those who live a life under the Rule of Saint Benedict and for those who would seek to live a life under the *influence* of the Rule of Saint Benedict. There is a sense in which I do have rules in common with each of the communities to which I am called and to whom I have been given, to which I am committed and within which I am to live a life that becomes the Gospel. But these rules govern only a portion and not all of my life. When it comes to the notion of a single rule for my life, the word *patchwork* comes to mind.

A part of my rule for worship and for service is shaped by and shared with the other members of the cathedral parish. Another part of my rule for prayer is held in common with some close friends. A part of my rule for work is shared with my wife and another part is shared with the editors and publishers who are kind enough to include me in their good work. But none of these common *rules* are written and none of them involves an abbot or an abbess. They are living, breathing rules, permeable and adjustable. They are no less rich and powerful and important because of their openness and adaptability. And the living in and out of these common rules is no less demanding.

"It takes heroic humility," writes Thomas Merton, "to be nothing more than the man and the artist that God intended you to be."

The sense of community we long for must be found within the context of scattered communities and unspoken rules. The sheer variety of such communities and rules demands humility, perhaps even humility on a heroic scale.

Humility is the basic posture from which we are able to do the work necessary to build and to live in community. Humility is required to get to obedience. And obedience, true obedience, is no less necessary in my communities than in monastic communities.

"The way to think of obedience," says spiritual director Elizabeth Canham, "is to think of it as another word for listening, really listening."

Humility is what creates the space within us—within our hearts and minds and souls and spirits—for obedience to grow. For real listening, humility is required, the kind of humility that says my will may not be the most important one. What may be most important is the will of the One Who made me. Or perhaps even the will of those around me, those to whom I am given and who have been given to me.

Humility is what is called for when I need to set what I want aside in order to better serve the needs of those around me. Humility is required to give myself up to a common rule in a marriage, in a home, in a business, in a congregation.

Humility is necessary for following the example of those who have gone before when what I want is to do what feels good to me, and to leave others to do as they please.

There are two other words—two other ways of being—that Benedict suggests will nurture the kind of humility that promises to deepen our life in community. This is the good news.

The bad news, of course, is they are not easy words.

Suffering is one of those words.

I do not believe Benedict is simply talking about the kind of suffering that comes from illness or tragedy or any other such circumstance. Such sorrows come to each of us in one way or another throughout our lives; there are lessons to be learned from enduring them, and no one wishes those lessons and the learning of them on anyone else.

But I believe there are also lessons to be learned from another way of looking at the word *suffering*.

Benedict recommends what I think of as selective suffering. If enough suffering does not land on you in the course of the woof and warp of your life, which will most likely be the case, you can find in Benedict's Rule suggestions for nurturing selective suffering in your life so as to have a healthy dose of it. Think of them as ways to help keep you humble along the way.

Benedict writes that we are always to be happy with the lowest and most menial treatment. By extension, we can assume we are to take the smallest piece, the worst seat in the house, the short end of the stick. None of which sounds like what we are taught these days. All of which require us to adopt a more humble posture in relationship to those around us.

From the earliest of our childhood days, the incessant drumbeat of our culture spurs us on to more and more—more education and more money, bigger houses and bigger cars, the best clothes and the best tables, and on and on.

To be sure, there is value in the sense of aspiration our culture instills in us. We all know stories of people who have achieved greatness, not only for themselves but also for others, as a result of striving to become more than what it appeared they were destined to be. And I do not for a moment imagine that in order to approach some sense of community, we are to set our sights lower when it comes to the work we are given to do and the people we have been dreamed into being by the One Who sent us here in the first place.

But from time to time the push to always be more and to get ahead can breed in us a certain kind of self-centeredness. We can find ourselves far too conscious of outdoing those around us or comparing ourselves with those we perceive to be above or below us. As a lifelong sports fan, I am as aware as anyone of the value of healthy competition on the playing field and in some other parts of our lives, but I also know that to compete for status or position with those who live down the block or in a better neighborhood is not always healthy. In some ways we will end up competing against our own sweet selves. The constant drive to be more and have more can be hard on our lives in community.

We are always looking for the best of everything, and yet Benedict challenges us to be happy with the lowest of everything. There are only two areas where anyone should be measured according to Benedict—good works and humility. And the latter calls for a life of less not more. Indeed, sometimes less is not more, sometimes less is everything.

———

Once he gets started, Saint Benedict goes a few steps further with his discussion of suffering.

He goes so far as to say we would do well to endure unjust or unfavorable conditions when they are put upon us and admonishes us to embrace our sufferings. Benedict believes Jesus meant what He said about our obligation to offer the other cheek when we have been struck a blow, offer our coat along with our shirt when we encounter someone in need, and offer to go two miles when we are forced to go one.

"Happy are they who are persecuted for the sake of the Gospel," Jesus said to a crowd on a hillside—a Gospel that includes turning the other cheek, giving away coats, and going extra miles. "Rejoice and be glad when it happens to you." In these words we encounter a deep truth that can change the texture and shape and depth and color and tone of our life together. A change for the better.

Deciding to take less rather than always striving for more, choosing to be last rather than always hurrying to be first, being willing to be the least among us rather than always needing to be the best among us—these all require us to become more humble, to make more room for others, to take others into account. And these acts of humility can nurture community in our lives.

———

Another word the Rule offers us to help in our pursuit of humility is *confession*.

Benedict tells his monks, applying the teaching long given to all of us by the Church, to make a habit of promptly and regularly confessing sinful thoughts and secret wrongs—to God, to superiors, to ones we have wronged. "Do not let the sun go down on your anger," writes Saint Paul, and I imagine he would advise the people in his community to not let the sun go down on their sins either. Carrying anger and nurturing community are difficult to do at the same time.

I have held on to anger and hurt or nursed a grudge too many times before not to recognize the wisdom of letting go of such baggage as soon as possible. I have also held on to my secret sins, hoping against hope those who were affected would not find out. I have often lived as though I would be able to keep them hidden and would not have to admit what I had done or thought, "the thoughts and deeds of which I am ashamed," as the Prayer of Confession refers to them. I have done so often enough to know that hiding sin and building community do not go together very well either.

I cannot speak for everyone, of course, but I am willing to venture a guess that I am not the only one who has ever held on to my anger or hidden my sins and has watched one or more of the communities to whom I have been given suffer as a result. And those sins, "known and unknown . . . things done and things left undone," as they are described in the Book of Common Prayer, can keep me from those with whom I am trying to find community. By contrast, honest, ongoing confession can help us nurture humility.

The way the word *confession* carries a notion of our confessing something we have done or not done is familiar to many of us. But there is another way of thinking about confession that can help us grow our humility as well.

"Every knee shall bow," writes Paul in his letter to his friends at Philippi, "and every tongue confess that Jesus Christ is Lord." Such a confession is not an admission of sin, it is an admission of who I am in relationship to someone or something else.

And the Rule calls for the monks to confess that they are worthless compared to others. To confess that we are less important than another is also to say that someone else is more important than we are. To make that confession—honestly and humbly—may begin to shape and change us, to help us treat others as though they are more than they may think they are, more than we think they are. This way of lifting each other up can only be good for our life together.

This call to confess that we are less than someone else—that someone else may be more important than we are—is jarring to our modern and Western sensibility, but there it is. I am not too surprised to read such an idea in the Rule; Benedict likes to remind us to remind ourselves every day we are going to die. He is not always the most cheerful of souls.

In response to Benedict's call to consider ourselves worthless, I need to say that I have been around enough children and enough people who suffer from depression and other troubles to know some of the dangers inherent in low self-esteem. (I have papers from my own time in the psych ward if anyone requires proof of the danger of low self-esteem.) A person's being told they are worthless by someone else—overtly or inadvertently—can lead to an unhealthy kind of confessing to one's worthlessness. I have to hold that knowledge in one hand while trying to hold the wisdom of the Rule in the other.

And the wisdom in the Rule to be found in this place—here where we are encouraged to confess our worthlessness—is simply that we need to recognize we are no more worthy than the next person. This recognition involves wisdom around which one can build a community.

Something happens at the moment I confess I am not the object of the exercise, at the moment I acknowledge that my happiness or joy or comfort is not the point, at the moment I admit I have no more right to any of the good things this sweet life we live together has to offer than the people to whom I have been given and who have been given to me. In that moment of humility, real and honest and true humility, I can begin to see and hear and live into and live out of the call of the Gospel—"Whoever exalts themselves will be humbled, and whoever humbles themselves will be exalted."

In such a moment, I think of Maundy Thursday and the priests washing the feet of parishioners who come forward. I think too of Ash Wednesday when the Church itself reminds us we are going to return to the dust from whence we came. And, astonishingly, these reminders make me grin. Partly because I can see the face of my sweet wife who loves these liturgies so much. And partly because I can catch a glimpse of the power that our embrace of humility and suffering and confession has—the power to make room for us to be drawn more closely to each other.

Khalil Gibran once wrote that "tears hollow out spaces in our hearts where joy can grow." Perhaps, in a similarly mysterious way, humility carves out little spaces in our hearts where love for others can grow.

"We are so used to hearing what we want to hear and remaining deaf to what it would be well for us to hear," writes Frederick Buechner, "that it is hard to break the habit."

Humility and all of the attendant words and phrases that come floating up when we say that word to ourselves—*less, quiet, modest, last, least, suffer, confess, admit*—are not the kind of words we typically associate with ourselves and the way we live our lives here in the twenty-first century. But a posture of humility is absolutely necessary for building community in the noisy and scattered and frenetic world in which we live. And anything feeding and nurturing a posture of humility—be it the washing of feet or the mark of ashes on a forehead, be it the confession of one's sins or the confession of one's unworthiness—should be seen as a gift.

Susan Muto writes, "In these days, spirituality is not a luxury, it is a necessity." I am coming to believe this is true about humility, too.

If we are to find a deeper sense of community, it may well be that some of us, all of us, need to be willing to humble ourselves. At least I think this is what Saint Benedict is saying to me these days. And so is the Christ he served, and the Mount's Sermon speaks directly to this.

Not too long ago, I was invited to speak to about sixty people who are part of the Academy for Spiritual Formation. These sixty had already been together for a year—meeting for a week each quarter—and would be together for another year on the same schedule.

In the evenings, the group's leadership team and the two speakers for the week would meet and process the events of the day and talk about logistical matters and the issues that had come up among the retreatants. One night, there materialized for me a lesson in instant community building that I did not even see coming. I took the lesson home with me for use in all of the communities of which I am a part.

That particular evening we got into an intense discussion about worship practices in different parts of the Church. There was a fair amount of back and forth and in making a comment, one person stepped on someone else's toes. It turned out the "step-er" had to leave the meeting early and when he later went to find the "step-ee" to apologize, he discovered that the step-ee had already gone to bed for the night. I know this because I was the step-er. And I know the step-ee had gone to bed because one of my friends in the group told me so when I explained I was seeking to apologize.

I went to bed worrying about what had happened.

The next morning at breakfast, the step-ee stopped by my table for about thirty seconds. My friend to whom I had confessed last evening had spoken to him, and he sought me out. The step-ee said this: "It does not matter at all. You are forgiven. Go worry about something else."

Which I promptly did, since being the speaker gives me plenty of stuff to worry about anyway.

Humble yourself. Suffer a little bit, selectively, perhaps. Confess, both your sins and how small and clumsy you may be from time to time.

If you do these things, community may happen.

A Ready Mercy

The One Who made us is merciful,
so we must be merciful, too.
—The Gospel of Our Lord

Imitate the loving example of the Good
Shepherd who left the ninety-nine sheep in the
mountains and went in search of the one sheep
that had strayed.

Exercise the utmost care and concern for
the wayward, because it is not the healthy that
need a physician, but the sick.

Always let mercy triumph over judgment so
that you too may win mercy. Remember not to
crush the bruised reed. Strive to be loved rather
than feared.
—From the Rule of Saint Benedict

Far too often in the history of Christianity theologians and teachers have given us another message, have dwelt on the unworthiness of men and women, their proneness to sin, their worthlessness. Yet there is none of this in Christ's teaching, nor in the Rule of St. Benedict.

—Esther de Waal

Humility helps us shift more and more of our focus away from ourselves and onto others within our communities. A posture of honest humility increases the likelihood that we will begin to really see and hear what is going on within and around those to whom we have been given and who have been given to us. And the more we look and listen, the more we can see the need to offer mercy to each other.

Ask anyone who is part of a community known as a family.

I was speaking with a neighbor the other day. We were talking about children, about my children and about the children she helped to raise at her house.

All of my children are older now and have moved away into homes of their own. Her children are gone now too. Both of our nests are empty. We laughed a little bit. Nests are supposed to empty, we both observed. I understand why some parents are less than thrilled when it happens at their nest. But I never quite understand why they seem so surprised.

I used to make my daughter promise me every year on her birthday she would stop growing up. I reminded her of this promise once when I visited her during the fall of her third year of college, at a coffee shop three hours away from where we raised her.

She grinned and told me she had been kidding all along. She was always going to grow up and have a life of her own some day.

I knew it all along, too, and simply did not want to admit it.

My neighbor and I fell to talking about another child, the young adult child of someone we know. This young man has had some struggles lately and has come home to regroup. He has made some mistakes, I understand, some of which he does not even want to talk about. Parents are not always sure what to do or say when their child, who is now a young adult, turns up at their door.

My neighbor said she thought the answer was easy. "You do the only thing you can do," she said. "Stand at the door with your arms open. Ask as few questions as is possible. Make no judgments. Say 'hello, we are so glad to see you.'"

I am reasonably certain she has never read Saint Benedict's Rule. But she knows what the saint knew. She knows what the Good Shepherd knows, and the father of the prodigal son, for that matter: "Always let mercy triumph over judgment."

Always be willing to leave the ninety and the nine. Always be ready to run down the road to greet the one who was lost.

"I desire mercy, not sacrifice, and if you knew what this saying means," says Jesus to those who would follow Him, "you would not condemn anyone. The One Who made us is merciful, so we must be merciful, too." Later He says to them, "The measure you give is the measure you will receive."

Perhaps if we give mercy, mercy will return to us. Perhaps when we need mercy the most.

I know two men who are brothers.

I also know they had a disagreement after their father died. It started out as a disagreement over a trivial matter and escalated quickly into a disagreement intense enough to open up some old and deep wounds and cause some new and painful ones. The whole episode took place in the span of only a couple of hours. The triviality of the initial disagreement notwithstanding, they have now not spoken to each other for years. And neither have their children nor their grandchildren spoken to the members of the other family. Whole stretches of their lives are going by without any contact between the two brothers— lives that are getting shorter, by the way. They both have less time to spend here on earth than they have already spent.

They used to be best of friends; I know, I saw them together. Now they cannot even speak because of the injury each believes he has suffered at the hands of the other. Even if they did suffer an injury, it was not much of one in the beginning. Now, however, the quarrel has become huge. If it were not so sad, it would be funny.

If these two men were the only ones I knew to whom this had happened, I might be tempted to laugh at them. Yet theirs is not the only story of people who have responded to injuries, real or perceived, with something less than the posture of mercy suggested by both the One Who came and the monk who wrote the Rule. These brothers are not the only ones who have chosen judgment rather than mercy. And the result has been sacrifice—a sacrifice of healing, a sacrifice of mercy, a sacrifice of good will, a sacrifice of community.

We all know a story like this in our family or at our work or in any of the other communities of our lives. We all have within us the capacity for behaving in just this way. We have all seen someone choose judgment over mercy.

For example, there is the guy I see in the mirror every morning.

I am perfectly capable, as we all are, of having my feelings hurt and my toes stepped on. And, of course, I am equally capable of hurting feelings and stepping on toes myself. And I have been here long enough to know that the people with whom such things can happen the quickest are those to whom I am the closest. I have also been here long enough to know that I am not the only one for whom this is true.

On occasion my response to being injured is to act as though someone in one of the communities to which I have been given got up in the morning and said, "I am going to do Robert in today. I am looking for an opportunity to make his life harder or to hurt his feelings or to treat him as less than the fine person he clearly is and has always been." Which may be a little over the top on my part.

More likely, someone in one of the crowds to whom I have been given has been clumsy. Or he has been under a particular pressure I may or may not know anything about. He was tired, he was hungry, he was distracted, he was overwhelmed. He had a job to do, he had bad news to bear, he had a budget to hit, he had a schedule to keep.

He did not set out to injure me, he just did. He did not set out to make my life harder or my sky darker, he just did. And in the wake of the injury, real or perceived, I have a choice: I can build community or I can break it down. I can respond in a way that makes for something more, something deeper and richer, or I can respond in a way that makes for something less.

The wisdom of the Rule is this: bear injuries patiently, do not repay one bad turn with another bad turn, do not act in anger or nurse a grudge. In short, act with mercy.

Pulling this off may require we learn to do another thing or two.

I had a fight with a friend. I remember the very place we were standing while yelling at each other, saying terrible stuff. We did not mean all of what we said, either one of us. What we did mean is that we were both so hurt and so frustrated, with each other and with ourselves, we could do no more than shout at each other. What exploded was our frustration at our combined inability to wrestle to the ground the difficulties that had built up between us over the years. What we chose was not mercy, and our choice affected not only him and me, but the rest of our family community as well, for years in fact.

Unfortunately, following the explosion we did what people do even though they know better—we proceeded to not speak to each other for a while. For almost twenty years. We were both perfectly justified, I suppose: the other had said terrible words, hurtful words. And we were able to manage our habits and patterns and associations so we did not have to run into each other anywhere. From time to time, someone in the family tried to trick us into being in the same room at the same time, but we were pretty good at avoiding it. We were not exactly enemies, but one would have been hard-pressed to tell the difference.

I told myself and the folks who knew the story and who inquired from time to time that I was perfectly willing to forgive him. All he had to do to move me from judgment to mercy was to come to me, admit how hateful he had been to me, own up to how much he had wronged me, and then say how much he wanted my forgiveness—even though he clearly did not deserve it. I would have forgiven him, of course, anytime in those twenty years. All he had to do was beg for mercy.

One day, I was at the cathedral for one of those ceremony things we so love and the Gospel broke out.

The story is too long to tell, but suffice it to say that in the space of a few minutes I forgave him. And he was not even in the room. Guess whose burden was lifted.

I have talked to enough people in my life to know I am not the only one who has ever held such weight in my heart— though I may be more gifted in this way than some. I have talked to enough people in my life to know I am not the only one who has lived for long stretches of time with an empty chair at the table, a house in the neighborhood that is avoided, an associate down the hall to whom one never speaks, a friend who one day just seems to have gone away.

I do not think—though I would love for this to be true—I am the only one who has ever failed to pray for my enemies, or failed to endure persecution for the sake of justice, or cursed someone when I should have been blessing them. I am not the only one whose first instinct when injured is something other than forgiveness.

And Benedict reminds me over and over again that community is maintained not because no one ever hurts anyone else, but because someone is willing to forgive.

Whatever you want to say about Benedict, his Rule attends to the Gospel. And the Gospel always leads us to where we began—mercy.

Mercy and humility go hand in hand. A certain amount of humility is needed to recognize that someone else's need for and hope for and desire for mercy in the face of their faults is no less important than your own desire for mercy in the face of your own faults. A certain amount of humility is necessary to come to grips with the fact that another's need to be forgiven and to be given a clean slate is as real and as valuable as your own when you come face-to-face with yet another moment in which you have fallen short of the glory of God—a relatively frequent occurrence in my life, and maybe in yours, too.

A certain amount of humility and wisdom is required as well in order to live with the notion that regardless of what people deserve—always deserve no matter what they have done—what people always have coming to them is mercy.

But all too often, when it comes to mercy, we act as though it is always better to receive than to give.

The more I listen to the Rule and the more I listen to the Gospel, the more I hear that mercy is not an occasional event, it is an ongoing stance. An ongoing stance that can bring about community rather than break it down.

Mercy is being always ready to bear the injuries that come your way. To bear them with grace and with courage. To bear them without complaint and without retaliation. To bear them with tolerance toward those who caused you injury, whether they did so intentionally or inadvertently. To bear them for the sake of a whole community.

Mercy is being always ready to forgive. Being ready to forgive whether the one who hurt you asks for forgiveness or not. Being ready to forgive instantly, before the sun goes down, even. Being ready to forgive for the sake of your own sweet self as well, being ready to free yourself from carrying the weight of anger and vindictiveness. Being ready to trade an act of mercy for the burden of a grudge.

A Wider Welcome

To welcome me is to welcome the One Who sent me.
—The Gospel of Our Lord

All who present themselves are to be welcomed as Christ, for he himself will say: I was a stranger and you welcomed me.

Great care and concern are to be shown in receiving poor people and pilgrims because in them more particularly Christ is received.
—From the Rule of Saint Benedict

I sometimes wonder if in the kingdom of heaven there is a great room, rather like a vast lost property office, filled with parcels of every shape and form, unclaimed blessing, that God has given us and we have failed to notice, to receive and make our own.
—Esther de Waal

Believing in something I cannot explain is something I do fairly often when it comes to the life of the Spirit. One of the things in which I believe these days is the hand-in-hand nature of the relationship between humility and mercy. And especially in the way these two working together begin to shape us.

Something about the way an honest humility and a more generous mercy work within us seems to affect the way that we see others, others with whom we are already in community and others to whom we may be being given.

Our sense of welcome can begin to deepen. And along with it our sense of community, present and potential, begins to deepen, too.

And our welcome begins to widen.

———

In a sense, I did not grow up in the little town where I grew up. What I mean is that in some sense I was *in* the town but not *of* the town.

We lived in a little town about thirty miles north of the city. My folks were born and raised in the city and most all of their friends came from one of two groups. Most were people who grew up in the same neighborhoods in East Nashville, went to the same high schools and college, and attended the same large Nazarene church their entire lives. The other group was made up of people from the religious music community with whom my father did business.

Between the two groups I met some of the finest people I have known, people who have become dear and gracious friends to me over the years. In many ways, the crowd was as good a crowd of folks as I may ever know, and my folks were lucky to have had this rich close group of friends for their whole lives. Having those friendships was a rare gift, the kind of gift we do not often see in the times in which we live. Frequent moves from one city to another, from one parish to another, from one job to another make it hard for such relationships to grow in today's world.

But looking back on those days I came to a realization about this community of friends.

For years, my father got up in the morning, dropped off his children at the bus stop or at one of the local schools, and headed off to the city for work. When we went to church—and we did so often—we would drive the same thirty miles back into the city to participate in a worship service or a prayer meeting or a Bible study or some other church activity with folks who lived thirty miles away. When we had company at the house, the company was made up of folks from the church or from the business.

The only actual neighbors who came to our house were relatives, some of whom lived on the same piece of property that we did. Or they were music business people, associates of my father, who had moved out to the little town. I have almost no memories of a crowd of folks from the neighborhood or down the street who ever came and sat on our patio or at our table or in our yard. People came to our house a lot, but they came from the city, not from down the road. The welcome mat was almost always out.

Growing up, I had a few friends on the basketball team, my "business" friends, if you will. And my parents hardly ever missed a game throughout my years of schoolboy basketball. They knew the parents of the other guys on the team and the cheerleaders and other folks who came to watch the small-town team play. High school football and basketball were big events in the town. But somehow, our real community was in the city, involving people with whom we went to church, did all the Christian stuff, and had *fellowship*—a word we only used in church, by the way.

My community was made up of people like me, and we would head to town to visit them as often as we could.

Welcoming the Stranger is only a mildly interesting theological discussion if you never actually meet one.

For those of us who are Church folks, those who like to talk about community and fellowship and the rest, the great risk is not that we will never find any sense of community in our lives, the risk is that we will spend half our lives driving across town to get it.

And even then we may not find community; we may only find a crowd of folks who are just like us. It could be that in a way we are only welcoming our own sweet selves. And it could be that community can be seen, maybe even should be seen, in a different light altogether—the light shed by the Rule.

One of those lights is geographic.

In monastic settings in Benedict's time, there was a sense in which the world was a smaller place. Most monks spent their whole lives in one place, rarely venturing beyond the walls, if at all. The community was a crowd of people made up of those you knew and lived with. The exceptions were guests and pilgrims and travelers who were welcomed into the community for brief periods of time.

This picture may still hold true in some cases, but the modern world clearly shapes certain aspects of today's monastic world. I know more than one nun who possesses a mobile telephone and an e-mail address and a website. Being a monk or a nun does not call for less engagement with the world, but rather a deeper engagement. The use of modern tools is nothing more than another way of being engaged.

For those of us who do not live as monks or nuns, one of the difficulties we face is the way we drive away to work, away to school, away to worship. The same is true for those who ride away to those places on a bus or a train.

The temptation is to keep driving until we find a community we like better than the one to which we have been given, the one that lives and moves and has its being in the neighborhood in which we live. But "all who present themselves are to be welcomed as Christ," Benedict writes.

The temptation is to merely wave at our community as we pass by on the way to a place where everyone on either side of the welcome mat is almost exactly like us. We do find community there, of course, and rightly so. What is perhaps not so right is that we often ignore rather than welcome the Christ Who lives next door or down the block or around the corner.

We are often so busy searching for community on the other side of town we fail to be truly present to the one in which we live. We are often so intent on building community where we work, we fail to notice the people around us. We are often so anxious to find a community of like-minded folks around whom we can feel comfortable, we fail to greet the Christ in the stranger we meet or in the neighbor whose name we cannot remember.

I wonder sometimes what keeps me from opening my arms a little wider and offering welcome to some folks who are not like me. Do I only want to agree with people instead of being engaged with people? Do I want to hang on to all of my treasured points of view and not have any of them challenged? Am I afraid I will be asked to do something harder or messier than I want to do? Am I fearfully ignoring the naked and hungry and thirsty Christ down the street in the name of heading across town to be with the people of God?

A priest once told me he thought the opposite of love was not hate. "The opposite of love," he said, "is fear." Fear can be just as hard on welcome. Hospitable is a difficult posture if you cannot let go of your fears and hold out your hands. Opening your hands to receive anyone at all is impossible while your fists are holding on to your positions so tightly your knuckles have turned white.

"Great care and concern," Benedict writes, "are to be shown in receiving poor people and pilgrims because in them more particularly Christ is received."

The Rule continues: "Show every respect for the sick, for children, for guests and for the poor. They must be truly served as though they were Christ because, as Christ says, 'What you did for one of these least you did for me.'"

This particular bit of the Gospel, thanks to the good Saint Benedict, breaks out on me in a couple of different ways these days.

The first is a close-to-home sort of way. The Gospel reminds me there is no shortage of places within blocks of my house where I am to welcome the Christ. Indeed, my street is only four blocks long, and there are new people along the street that I do not know. But within these four blocks I do know there are at least three alcoholics, a schizophrenic, a drug addict, and four individuals who struggle with serious bouts of depression. There are also three single mothers, and maybe a dozen school children. One of the school children has a disability and another has been in trouble with the police. There are five older folks whose health is not good. And these are only the people I know about.

In my travels around the country I have people tell me of their struggles. They need to tell someone their troubles, someone who will not tell anyone else, someone who will not judge, someone who will not let their secrets out—someone not of their community, interestingly enough. I am happy to help.

What I have learned most from these conversations is this: what many of us carry around that other people in our communities do not know is astonishing. The unseen and unknown burdens many of us bear break my heart. There is no telling what I do not know about the people who live up and down my street.

But I know enough to know at least this: great care and concern must be shown for all, for whatever I do to and for anyone, whether they are least or most or in between, I do to and for the Christ.

And my four blocks are not the only place one can find folks who are young and old, guests and pilgrims. My four blocks are not the only four blocks where there are sick to be cared for and strangers to be welcomed. Your four blocks or your apartment building or your subdivision also needs folks whose hands are out in welcome.

A priest from Detroit who was a dear friend of mine used to say that for every hour we spend with Jesus in our prayers, we should spend an hour with Jesus among the poor—the poor of spirit and the poor of heart, those in poverty and in distress, those without homes and without hope. This Jesus is never very far away from us, down the street or down the block or across the hall or across the room.

———

There is another way in which the Gospel's call for welcoming the stranger is speaking to me these days.

And it is saying something to me that none of the four Gospel writers nor a sixth-century monk—nor most of us, now that I think of it—could ever have imagined: all of my communities and all of your communities are connected to everyone else's communities these days.

I know you know this—the signs are everywhere. And if you missed the signs yesterday, there will be new signs today and tomorrow. And some portion of the new signs will come to you electronically. They will bring with them more strangers for whom you may need to find a sense of welcome in your heart—even if you never see those strangers face-to-face.

These days I am trying to decide if I think the world has gotten smaller or larger.

On the one hand, somewhere between jet airplanes and mobile telephones, the twenty-four-hour news cycle and the World Wide Web, the digital camera and the satellite image, the world seems to have shrunk. I can see a news bulletin about a cyclone on the other side of the world and watch in real time as the survivors come stumbling out from under the clouds. I can get a note in the mail from a young woman working in the Peace Corps in Uganda and be at my computer within minutes, looking at pictures of the village where she works. I can hear of a friend who has fallen ill overseas and get a telephone update on her condition every afternoon.

Suddenly, Uganda is not so far away after all. And neither is Baghdad or Beijing, Malaysia or Mexico City, San Juan or San Francisco.

But even as the world seems smaller, it also seems more vast and more full, richer and broader and deeper and wider than ever before. The world did not seem like such a large place back when I lived a life bound between America's two bordering oceans.

But now the world seems huge to me. Suddenly it has to be large enough to hold all of China and India, the places where almost half of all humanity lives, the half many of us never took into account before. The world has to be large enough for those people who were hidden behind the Iron Curtain for so long. The world has to be large enough for the peoples of the developing world, a world that is not quite so easily unseen, not quite so easily unknown, not quite so easily ignored as it was a few years ago, back when the earth was smaller or larger or whichever it was.

Are all these people part of the community to whom I have been given and who is being given to me? Am I to welcome them too? Or can I look the other way when the pictures come into view?

Holding these notions—the sense of the world being somehow smaller and larger at the same time, the sense of being called to somehow grasp that a whole world of people are a part of my community now, and the sense of needing to somehow live a life that welcomes them into mine—in my head and my heart is not always easy to do. But living within the bounds of paradox is not uncommon in any life of faith, not if we are honest with ourselves and each other and the One in Whom we have believed. One of the first questions of a faithful follower is this: is God within me or without me?

The answer is yes, of course, and we are off on our mysterious journey in the direction of the One Who made us, the One Who will welcome us home.

Strangely enough, the world being both smaller and larger at the same time is not what I am struck by these days. What I am struck by these days is that the crowd of people who have been given to me and to whom I have been given has gotten a fair amount larger.

How much water I use affects the lives and the livelihoods of people hundreds and thousands of miles away. How far a fish travels before I take it off the shelf of the local grocery store and put it on the grill in my backyard suddenly has to be seen in the light of how that travel has affected folks I will never even meet. Where I spend my money and where the products that I buy have come from suddenly matters. My use of oil in all of its various forms, from the materials used to make the instrument with which I am writing this book to the machines used to bring the book to your door, suddenly matters.

A little bit of humility suggests that I may not have more right to some of these resources than others do, regardless of where I or they live. A hint of mercy reminds me that others are as much in need as I am, if not more so. A modicum of welcome and hospitality helps me to see that opening my hands and arms enough to stop grasping everything within reach may allow strangers I perhaps will never see—in other parts of my city, my country, my world—to find the world a more welcoming and hospitable place.

Once I begin to catch a glimpse of my connectedness to others across the world, everything has to be held up into the light of this growing sense of larger community. How much gasoline I use, whether or not I recycle, how I vote, where I buy my vegetables—all these choices matter. These choices may involve small decisions, but acts of hospitality and welcome are often simple and quiet and small. And these simple acts and small decisions matter not only to me, they matter to this larger community of which I am newly aware and suddenly, astonishingly, and clearly a part.

We have been a part of this larger community for longer than we know, of course. Or for longer than we have been willing to admit. Now that we know better, our past claim of ignorance—both in the sense of our not knowing and of our not paying attention to what we have learned—is no longer a particularly wise position to hold. Ignorance is certainly not a very good claim to make in the light of sentences like these from the Rule: "Let us serve one another." "Let us compete in doing good works." "Let us welcome the stranger."

—

According to the Rule, monks are to take turns serving one another at mealtimes. No one should be excused from such menial work, which, on the surface, is hardly an earth-changing principle. Cooking a meal and setting the table and clearing, washing, and putting away the dishes are ordinary bits of our days. I grin at the passages about mealtimes every time I read them because the emphasis on the ordinary does not seem to speak to lofty spiritual questions. But the ordinariness does speak to me about the way we are to open our arms to each other.

I think the core wisdom of the Rule concerns the admonition to serve one another. Our service to one another—at table, in the office, down the hall, or down the block—is a way to be reminded that one person is no more or less important than another. It is a reminder that it is in the ordinary of our lives that we begin to find the proper posture from which to build community. A reminder that we are to always open our arms in welcome and hospitality to one another.

And one another means all of the one anothers in all of the communities to which I have been given. Not simply the one anothers I head toward when I myself want to feel the most welcome. Or the one anothers where welcome is easy because we are all the same. Or the one anothers whose zip code or denominational affiliation is the same as mine. Or the one anothers who look like me and whose language is the same as mine and whose flag is red, white, and blue.

Welcome that is only wide enough for those like me is welcome, to be sure, but it is not as wide as it might be. And probably not as wide a welcome as the One Who made us is hoping we will learn to offer.

———

We have to be careful we do not isolate ourselves.

We have to be careful we do not give in to the temptation to seek and create community in ways that exclude rather than welcome the stranger. It is not hard to be in fellowship with those who are not different from us. Nor is it hard to push the stranger away without realizing it.

We have to be careful, too, we are not so caught up in the search for the Christ in the place across town where we work or worship that we fail to see the Christ down the street or at our door or downstairs in the parlor or at the table during mealtime. We have to be sure to pay careful attention to the poor and the young and the pilgrim and the elderly and the sick. We have to be sure we watch for and welcome the Christ within them when He is presented to us.

We have to be careful to remember we are part of larger communities, far larger than some of us have ever realized before, communities made up of people we are not likely to ever meet, comprising cities and states, countries and continents—a planet full of folks, to tell the truth. We have to be sure that whenever the opportunity presents itself, our actions in response originate from a place of humility and mercy and welcome.

We have to take care, too, that we do not forget that serving one another is at the heart of any hope for finding and nurturing community, in any of the communities to which we are given. And serving one another is what we are called to do—no matter how near or far those one anothers may be or how like or unlike us they are, no matter whether we see them each day or each week or never at all.

——

Being shy is not helpful when I am trying to wrap my arms around all of those to whom I am being given these days.

I think about them all—my family and my neighbors, the crowd of folks I work with, my fellow parishioners scattered all over town. Then I think of the community of folks I stumbled into when I attended the Academy for Spiritual Formation and this brings to mind the larger Anglican communion of which I am a part. I think about the part of the city I live in and the city as a whole.

The list goes on and on. More and more of my conversations with friends and fellow pilgrims include words like *global* and *international*. More and more places like Darfur and Myanmar and Belize and Tbilisi are mentioned. More and more I find it harder and harder to ignore the poor around me, whatever the reason for or source or manifestation of their poverty. More and more I wonder how I fit into this ever growing and ever shrinking world we live in.

I wonder about all of this even as I set the table or fold the laundry for one community, as I head to a backyard down the street to grill out with a neighbor, as I head to the cathedral for one of the ceremonies we love, as I open up the *New York Times* and see pictures from some spot in the world I have never heard of.

"I was a stranger and you welcomed me," is what I remember. And that stranger and this welcome are what matters.

The Act of Caring

Whoever gives even as much as a cup of cold water to the least of their neighbors can expect to receive the reward of the faithful.
—The Gospel of Our Lord

Show every concern for the sick, for children, for guests and for the poor.

Care of the sick must rank above and before all else, so that they may be truly served as Christ, for he said, "I was sick and you visited me," and, "What you did for one of these least brothers you did for me."
—From the Rule of Saint Benedict

We are being asked to become transforming agents within human society rather than revolutionary ones acting outside it.
—Esther de Waal

In the fourth century, as more and more monastic communities began to develop across the Christian world, the Church called upon these communities to become more than houses for prayer. They were to become houses of hospitality and healing, too.

As written in the Rule, pilgrims and guests were to be welcomed "as Christ himself." Hence the long tradition of hospitality encountered by anyone who has visited a monastery governed by Benedict's Rule.

According to the Church fathers, particular attention was to be given to caring for the sick. From the earliest days of the Church, as one can read in Justin the Martyr's letter, there was an emphasis on caring for the sick, the widows, the orphans, the needy, as well as strangers on a journey. Not only were monks and nuns to care for their own but for all those who came to them in need as well.

And those who have been given to us and to whom we have been given need us not only to care, but also to show that we do.

———

We were invited to a wedding in New Orleans the February after Hurricane Katrina had come through the city. The wedding was a joyous affair, held on a clear, cool, crisp Louisiana day. Joy was hard to come by in New Orleans in those days, and still is on many days.

We went because Frank and Betty were about to see their son Jack joined in matrimony to the girl who loved him the most. The two young people had been together off and on for eight or ten years, but Frank and Betty had sensed all along she was the only girl for their only child.

Betty had not been feeling well and had gone to the doctor a few weeks before the wedding. She told us later the doctor had called on the day before she left home to travel south to New Orleans for the festivities to say he needed to see her. He was using his "the test results are not so good" voice. Whatever the news was, she told him, it would have to wait until after the wedding. She was going to New Orleans to celebrate, and whatever had to be faced would have to be faced when she got back home.

The news was not good, and the word *cancer* came upon them, followed by other words—*surgery* and *chemotherapy* and *radiation* and all the rest.

Frank and Betty had grown up and made their home in the same small Delta town in Mississippi. She had worked at the local bank for what seemed like forever, and Frank had run a small business in the town for almost as long. But though a lot of people knew them, they lived private lives. Betty's closest friends were Anne and Carol, whom she had known since grade school.

Betty did not want to spend the last days she had left anywhere but home. And home was a small apartment they had built some years before up over Frank's business.

So the last four or five weeks of Betty's life were hard for her and for everyone else, especially Frank. He was doing his best to care for Betty upstairs, keep his business going downstairs, and come to grips in between with the fact he was about to lose the woman to whom he had been married for almost forty years.

And it was hard for Jack, who kept making the six-hour drive from New Orleans as often as he could to be with his mom. Betty was wasting away before their eyes—and before her own eyes, too, on the rare days she could stand up and get to the mirror and have a look.

So without much ceremony at all, Anne and Carol put their own lives on hold, moved in, and took over. They arranged for food and took turns sleeping on the couch so there would be someone who could help Frank care for Betty in the middle of the night. They made the rounds back and forth to the doctor and picked up prescriptions and changed bed linens. They stayed out of sight when they needed to and kept people away when Frank and Betty wanted to be left alone. They ran the vacuum and took out the trash and updated the relatives and friends.

When the end drew near—too soon, less than eight months after the wedding—Anne and Carol showed Frank and Jack how to lie down beside Betty and hold her close until she was gone. Then they went into the other room until Frank and Jack told them the time had come. And then they made the calls and the word went forth and the rest of us descended upon the little town.

By the time we all got there, Anne and Carol had called the mortuary and had written the obituary and were working on the condolence book. They were taking in casseroles and being patient with relatives and keeping an eye on Frank and Jack.

And then they were gone, back to their own lives, the lives they had put on hold or managed from afar for those few weeks. I know from Frank and Jack, though, that Anne and Carol still keep tabs on them.

There is an old prayer that ends "and may your holy angels bring us peace," and every time I hear it prayed I think of Anne and Carol.

This story is a fine example of what caring for others within community looks like. But this is not the only story I know that has that look.

I remember the way people in my neighborhood began to gather around a couple on the night their son died. He was a freshman attending college a few hours away, and when the news came that he was gone and by his own hand, it did not take long for a crowd to gather at this couple's house. Some of the neighbors came off and on and went back and forth for days doing as much as they could to help.

I think of the folks who kept a little girl while her mother suffered through another pregnancy, one so hard she was bedridden for months.

I am reminded of a friend out East who has put his career on hold for some time now while taking care of his aging parents. He writes from time to time to say that the life he is living is hard most days, but he is hanging on.

We all know stories like these. We all have been part of these stories ourselves. Families and neighbors and parishes gather around the sick and the needy all the time. Something happens to someone we know, the word goes forth, and the next thing you know, a crowd has gathered. Someone is taking care of the meals and someone else is making the telephone calls. Someone turns up to watch the children when they need to be watched and someone else drives the sick person to the doctor.

That these painful struggles happen to us and those to whom we are given is not a surprise. Life is always unpredictable and not always kind. I am also not surprised people respond in the way they do. People want to help, and their hearts go out to those they love.

One of the things that *is* surprising is that we do not always recognize these acts of caring for one another as part of our spiritual practice. In all humility, by any sense of the word *mercy*, with as much welcome as we can muster, we are to care for each other—and especially when we are sick and alone and struggling and hopeless, whatever the attendant circumstances may be.

Also surprising for me is that we do not always recognize just how much our caring for each other can do to make us one with each other. Our caring for each other—when we are sick, when we are discouraged, when we are lost, when we are needy—is perhaps one of the most powerful affirmations of our life together we can find.

There are moments in my life of great joy and wonder that I have shared with people whom I am close to. I think of such times as days in which the sun has never quite set; they are golden still, in my memory at least. I remember who stood beside me on those days and I am grateful for those people and for the moments of joy we shared.

But the people for whom I am most grateful and to whom I may well be the closest are the ones who have shared the darker days of our lives. Whether they are people I see weekly or rarely or no longer at all, the truth is that our being there and with and for and beside each other when one of us was sick or hurting or in pain has bound us together deeply, perhaps more deeply than any joy can.

Something about being naked and hungry and thirsty before each other, something about being clothing and food and drink for each other—something about being those things can make us one with Christ and one with each other.

———

Our acts of caring for each other need not always be heroic for them to deepen our community. In some ways the words *hungry* and *naked* and *thirsty* can cover a lot of ground. You fed me, clothed me, and gave me drink can cover a lot of ground, too. Ground that includes a wide range of both places of need and acts of caring.

I am thinking now of a man who used to live on our street. He was in his eighties, long retired, and got up every morning from Monday through Friday and drove off somewhere for the day. I asked once where he went all day. His answer made me grin. "I deliver groceries to old people," he said with a grin of his own, as though he was still a young man.

I am thinking of a woman I know who married in her late thirties, and when the job she had was no longer there, she was financially able to stay home. She did not stay there for long. She started volunteering a couple of days a week at a hospital, sitting and talking with families of seriously ill patients. The years have gone by, twenty of them almost, and now she runs part of the volunteer program.

A filmmaker I know saw a story in the paper about some men on death row at a nearby state prison, men who were writing poems and stories about life before prison and life inside. One day the filmmaker went to visit one of these prisoners. He goes to the prison regularly now, taking along writers to meet with the writing class there.

You know people like these too.

We all know people who work in homeless shelters and run the Room in the Inn program in their local parish. We know people who collect coats to give away and gather up canned goods for the local food bank. We know people who keep an eye out for the older couple that lives across the street, the couple whose kids have grown and moved far away and who need a hand with the groceries or some other chore from time to time, having nowhere to turn. We know people who take young children to the park for an hour so a young mother can have a few moments of quiet in an otherwise packed day. We know people who teach others how to read.

Not only do you know such folks, you are probably even one of them from time to time, maybe even more often than you give yourself credit for.

Whatever the circumstances, the moments when we are being the Christ to the Christ Who needs our attention, our care, our help are the moments in which we become one with each other. These are the moments when our life together grows richer and deeper. These are the moments we approach communion with each other. These acts of caring, large and small, create little places in our hearts where community can grow.

Perhaps it takes these moments and these acts for our joy to be complete.

Living for Others

You must do for others as you would have them do for you.
—The Gospel of Our Lord

*Are you hastening toward your heavenly home?
Then with Christ's help, keep a little rule that is
written for beginners.*

*After that, you can set out for loftier summits
of the teaching and the virtues, and under God's
protection you will reach them.*

*Do not aspire to be called holy before you
really are, but first be holy that you may more
truly be called so.*

And never lose hope in God's mercy.
—From the Rule of Saint Benedict

*St. Benedict is not looking for anything
spectacular or unusual. He is asking us to
sanctify the present moment. . . .*
—Esther de Waal

Annie Dillard writes, "How we spend our days is, of course, how we spend our lives. What we do with this hour, and that one, is what we are doing."

I laughed out loud the first time I read those two sentences. I still smile whenever I think of them. In fact, the sentences made me grin when I wrote them down just now.

Some would say Ms. Dillard is merely stating the obvious. They are right, of course. But I think she is reminding me of something more. I think she is reminding me to not get so caught up in wrestling with the complexities of my life that I miss the simple facts of my life. And maybe even miss the point of it in the process. I think she is reminding me to pay attention to each hour, know it for what it is, be present to it so that I miss as little as possible, and spend it as wisely as I can.

I spend my life an hour at a time. How I spend my hours is how I spend my life.

Whom I spend them with and whom I spend them for are the communities to whom I have been given and who have been given to me. How I am with them—with this person and that one, in this moment and the next—either makes our life together richer or poorer. What I say and do next will either make our communion deeper and wider or miss a chance to do those things. Or worse, I may do something to make our communion less than it was a few moments ago.

All of which seems so simple I wonder why I do not always remember to remember it.

———

Life in our time can be complex. And the nature of the way we move in and out of the communities to which we belong can make actually being present to them a bit complex, too.

We work with one set of people and worship with another, we live with one crowd of folks and are neighbors with another. Sometimes there is still another set we socialize with or are with because our children go to the same school or play ball together.

We long to know and be known, to be deeply and richly in community, and this is hard to do given the way we come in and out of each other's lives. We know some about each other, but sometimes there is much more unknown than known.

The distances we travel to work or to church can make being with a particular community difficult. The pace of our work and the busyness encouraged by our church's programs often limit the chances to simply be present to one another in a way that allows us to really know each other.

I long for a deeper sense of community and getting there seems to be more than I can accomplish.

———

There are two little girls who live down the block from us and they are off to kindergarten this year. The little girls are friends of ours and so are their folks.

Our children have long been out of school—and out of the house—so I have not been around kindergartners in a while.

But because we do know these two, I have been privy to some of the uneasiness associated with their going off to school for the first time. These are bright and talented little girls who are going to do just fine in school. And most days as the summer was winding down, they were excited about the notion of going to school.

We heard full reports on the day they went to buy school uniforms. Then we heard about the day they went to buy school supplies. I was a little envious of those stories, for I love looking at paper and pens. (I could use some new crayons, too, come to think of it.)

But we also heard some of the anxiety. Once, at a park outing we shared with the two families, we heard this plaintive little moan: "But I can't go to school yet, I am only five." After a couple of years of waiting to turn five so she could go off to school, the girl realized she might be able to get *out* of going to school by claiming she was too young.

We also heard one of the little girls say through apprehensive tears, "But I can't read."

I wanted to sit down next to them both and say everything was going to be okay. I wanted to tell them to worry about the simple stuff: Wear your uniform. Tie your shoes. Take your books. Sit down and be quiet when you are supposed to. Raise your hand before you talk in class. Be nice to the other kids. You are going to get the hang of this. You will be fine.

Part of the power of the Rule of Saint Benedict is its insistence on reminding us of what we already know to be true and yet somehow fail to keep in front of us as we go about our daily lives.

"Honor everyone, and never do to another what you would not want done to yourself," we read in the Rule. "Love your neighbor as yourself," we read in the Gospel.

Such sentences sound so childlike that when we hear them we sometimes grin with a "my, my, what a sweet thing to say" sort of look on our face and press on with life in the real world. And while we are busy hustling and bustling our way through our complicated lives, we wonder why we sometimes seem so alone.

———

Remember the simple stuff is what I hear when I am reading the Rule.

Whoever exalts himself shall be humbled, and whoever humbles himself shall be exalted. Remember that what someone else wants to have happen next is as valuable as what you want to have happen next, maybe even more so. Remember to listen, really listen. Remember who you are in relation to others and to the One Who made you. Be willing to take less, to be the last.

Always let mercy triumph over judgment. Do not damage a bruised reed. You cannot build community with a hardened heart or a closed fist. Do not repay a bad turn with another bad turn. Turn the other cheek. Go another mile. Forgive each other. The measure you give is the measure you will receive.

All who present themselves are to be welcomed as Christ. The world is smaller than it used to be. The world is larger than it used to be. You must be open to each other and to the One Who made us. Open to the good and the bad of life with others, open to the ups and the downs, the gains and the losses. Open to treating others the way you want to be treated.

Whoever gives even as much as a cup of cold water to the least of their neighbors can expect to receive the reward of the faithful. See who is being given to you and to whom you are being given. Care of the sick must come before all else. Let all serve one another in love.

These are the simple things. They are not, however, necessarily easy things to do. Which is why the Rule reminds us of another simple thing: *What is not possible to us by nature, ask the Lord to supply by grace.*

———

Our life together, our life in community, is not always an easy concept to get our hands and hearts and heads around. The nature of community in our age seems so different than it was for the ones who went before us.

But this fact does not lessen the desire we have to live in some deeper and wider sense of community with others. We, even the shy ones like me, do not want to be alone. We were not made to live that way. The desire to know others and be known by others—deeply and honestly and openly—is a part of the image of the One Who made us, a part of the image in which we were made.

Our hunger for community is no more likely to go away than is our need for work or our need for rest or our need to connect through prayer to the One Who made us this way.

The call to keep the two commandments that fulfill all of the Law and all of the Prophets is not going to go away either. It too is a simple call to us, though neither of the two commandments is necessarily easy to fulfill.

———

At the beginning of the Rule are these words: "Therefore we intend to establish a school for the Lord's service." The *school* for the Lord's service that I attend is different than the one for which the Rule was written.

But there is much to learn from the wisdom of the Rule about humility and mercy, welcome and caring. There is much to learn here about living a life in community, no matter what the communities in our lives look like. There is much more wisdom to be learned here than I have learned so far in my life.

I am too old for kindergarten now, and maybe even too old to be called a beginner anymore, yet when it comes to the life of the Spirit, I feel as though I am just beginning.

Perhaps another year in the school for the Lord's service will do me very good. Perhaps I can learn to love God and my neighbor—the One Who made me and the ones to whom I have been given—more deeply.

A Note About Saint Benedict

Before Benedict was a saint, he was a monk.

Benedict was born to wealthy parents in Nursia; from there his family moved to Rome when he was boy so he could attend school. This was during the reign of Theodoric of the Ostrogoths (493–526). Rome was peaceful then, even though the previous century had seen the city sacked on two occasions by barbarians. In the midst of the relative peace of the times, paganism began to rise, and Benedict became disgusted by what he saw and made a choice to leave the city, renounce the world, and live as a solitary in a cave near a town called Subiaco, some thirty miles east of Rome.

As time passed, Benedict came to the attention of those who lived nearby and began to acquire some reputation as a holy man. At some point a group of monks asked him to be their abbot, a position he reportedly took on with some reluctance. His reluctance proved to be well-founded, as the same group of monks later tried to poison him. (Monastery life is filled with more intrigue than one would imagine.)

Benedict headed back to his cave. Not long afterward, another group of monks came to join him, and together they eventually established twelve monasteries comprised of twelve monks each.

After a time, troubles arose with the local clergy, and Benedict took several disciples and moved nearly eighty miles south of Rome to a mountaintop, where he founded the monastery at Monte Cassino. He lived there until his death around 547. At the time of his death, his fame as a holy person had spread to the degree that even kings came to visit and seek his counsel.

The Rule he wrote to regulate the lives of the monks under his care has become the focal point for Christian monastic life in the years since.

———

Some years ago now, a friend of mine suggested I read the Rule. He thought that if I was serious about living a life of prayer, there might be some wisdom to be found in the traditions and practices of a crowd of folks who had been living such lives for centuries.

The suggestion made some sense to me, of course, even though the life of a monk is different than mine in many ways. I read the Rule through one time and have been trying to recover ever since. Even though I am not called to live the life of a monk, I am called to live a life that becomes the Gospel. I too am called to pray without ceasing.

In my first few minutes of reading, in the preface to the edition of the Rule I had bought, I came across some powerful lines from the writer Thomas More, who had himself lived a large portion of his life under the Rule.

More writes that practicing the core parts of the Rule can "give life a special quality, a tranquility and calm that are difficult or impossible to find in the non-monastic world. In the midst of our busy lives we can practice the spirit of this rule."

Those words spoke to a longing in my heart the first time I read them. They still do.

What is the spirit of the Rule, I began to wonder, and how can I live under the influence of that spirit?

Some writing is alive, it lives and breathes, it works its way into your heart and soul and mind. The words are not ever quite the same whenever you go back to them; they somehow build on themselves. The writing shapes and changes and transforms you.

We all have books that affect us like that. Saint Benedict's Rule is one of those books for me.

Perhaps you will discover the Rule to be the same for you.

Notes on Books

There are some books I have leaned on in writing this book, and have been leaning on for years, now that I think of it.

The Scripture epigraphs, and any other Scripture quoted in the book, are an author's paraphrase based on *The New English Bible*. This Bible was first published by Oxford University Press, before being revised in the 1980s and renamed the *Revised English Bible*. The original version can be found through used booksellers.

The epigraphs from the Rule of Saint Benedict are either quoted directly from or are an author's paraphrase from my favorite translation of the Rule—the Vintage Spiritual Classics edition, Timothy Fry, OSB, editor. It was published in 1998 by Random House of New York.

The epigraphs by Esther de Waal are from her fine book *Living With Contradiction*, a faithful companion to me and to many others.

Any liturgy has been quoted or adapted from the Book of Common Prayer.

The Oxford English Dictionary is where I turn to learn the origins and meanings of words.

Finally, there are some additional writers whose work I turn to again and again as I contemplate my life in light of the Rule of Saint Benedict. Some are more explicit than others about the Rule, but I have found that each of them, even those who do not discuss Benedict at all, somehow echo his wisdom.

I recommend them to you, as they too are fine companions for your journey.

Frederick Buechner, *The Sacred Journey*
Elizabeth J. Canham, *Heart Whispers*
Annie Dillard, *The Writing Life*
Louis Evely, *That Man Is You*
John McQuiston II, *Always We Begin Again*
Thomas Merton, *Thoughts in Solitude*
Henri Nouwen, *The Living Reminder*
Elizabeth O'Connor, *The Eighth Day of Creation*

Your favorite bookseller can help you find any and all of the above. I know because I keep buying copies of many of them to give away.

———

Study questions to accompany this book are available at www.paracletepress.com and robertbensonwriter.com. We will be glad to hear from you.

Author's Note

I want to say that some of the names in the book have been changed to protect the privacy of those mentioned.

I want to say that I am, as always, grateful to all of the people at Paraclete Press—especially Pamela, Jon, and Sister Mercy—for the chance to make a book at all. And for their particular grace throughout the sometimes difficult days that passed between this book's dreaming and its coming true.

I want to say thank you much to Ms. Lil of Dorchester Lane, the leading member of the Order of the Red Pen. The famed critic Clive Barnes once said of his work, "The job's impossible and one must pray that one will be only moderately incompetent." I feel the same about my own work, and if I manage to rise to even moderately incompetent, it is generally because of both her hard work and her gentle spirit.

I also want to declare once again that I am more grateful than I am poet enough to say, for everything, for always, to Ms. Jones of Merigold.

ABOUT PARACLETE PRESS

WHO WE ARE

Paraclete Press is a publisher of books, recordings, and DVDs on Christian spirituality. Our publishing represents a full expression of Christian belief and practice—from Catholic to Evangelical, from Protestant to Orthodox.

We are the publishing arm of the Community of Jesus, an ecumenical monastic community in the Benedictine tradition. As such, we are uniquely positioned in the marketplace without connection to a large corporation and with informal relationships to many branches and denominations of faith.

WHAT WE ARE DOING

PARACLETE PRESS BOOKS | Paraclete publishes books that show the richness and depth of what it means to be Christian. Although Benedictine spirituality is at the heart of all that we do, we publish books that reflect the Christian experience across many cultures, time periods, and houses of worship. We publish books that nourish the vibrant life of the church and its people.

We have several different series, including the best-selling Paraclete Essentials and Paraclete Giants series of classic texts in contemporary English; Voices from the Monastery—men and women monastics writing about living a spiritual life today; award-winning poetry; best-selling gift books for children on the occasions of baptism and first communion; and the Active Prayer Series that brings creativity and liveliness to any life of prayer.

MOUNT TABOR BOOKS | Paraclete's newest series, Mount Tabor Books, focuses on liturgical worship, art and art history, ecumenism, and the first millennium church, and was created in conjunction with the Mount Tabor Ecumenical Centre for Art and Spirituality in Barga, Italy.

PARACLETE RECORDINGS | From Gregorian chant to contemporary American choral works, our recordings celebrate the best of sacred choral music composed through the centuries that create a space for heaven and earth to intersect. Paraclete Recordings is the record label representing the internationally acclaimed choir Gloriæ Dei Cantores, praised for their "rapt and fathomless spiritual intensity" by *American Record Guide*; the Gloriæ Dei Cantores Schola, specializing in the study and performance of Gregorian chant; and the other instrumental artists of the Gloriæ Dei Artes Foundation.

Paraclete Press is also privileged to be the exclusive North American distributor of the recordings of the Monastic Choir of St. Peter's Abbey in Solesmes, France, long considered to be a leading authority on Gregorian chant.

PARACLETE VIDEO | Our DVDs offer spiritual help, healing, and biblical guidance for a broad range of life issues including grief and loss, marriage, forgiveness, facing death, bullying, addictions, Alzheimer's, and spiritual formation.

Learn more about us at our website:
www.paracletepress.com or phone us
toll-free at 1.800.451.5006

SCAN
TO
READ
MORE

You may also be interested in . . .

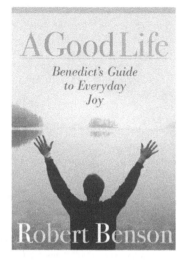

REFLECTING ON WHAT MAKES A "GOOD LIFE," Robert Benson offers a warmhearted guide to enriching our lives with the wisdom of Benedict. Each chapter is shaped around a Benedictine principle: prayer, rest, community, and work, and explores the timeless, practical ways that Benedictine spirituality can shape our lives today.

ISBN: 978-1-55725-449-8
$14.99, Paperback

IN TODAY'S HECTIC, CHANGING WORLD, being an oblate offers a rich spiritual connection to the stability and wisdom of monastic life. In this essential guide, Brother Benet Tvedten explains how people who live and work in "the world" are still invited to balance work with prayer, cultivate community with others, and otherwise practice their spirituality like monks.

ISBN: 978-1-61261-414-4
$14.99, Paperback

Available from most booksellers or through Paraclete Press
www.paracletepress.com; 1-800-451-5006
Try your local bookstore first.